DEDICATION

This edition is dedicated to Wright Langley (1935-2000) of Key West. He was a photographer, historian, journalist, publisher and civic leader. He will be missed!

Ernest
Hemingway
In
Key West

A Guide

By Marsha Bellavance-Johnson
with Lee Bellavance
Illustrated by Allison Gosney

Published by
THE COMPUTER LAB
Ketchum, Idaho

FAMOUS FOOTSTEPS™

guide booklets
about famous people
in their favorite places

Front cover photo:
    Ernest Hemingway at the wheel of *Pilar*, probably mid-1930's. Courtesy of the John F. Kennedy Library.

Back cover photo:
    Ernest Hemingway with his first born son, John, called Jack, nicknamed "Bumby", on the docks in Key West, late 1920's. Courtesy of Jack Hemingway.

Library of Congress Control Number: 00-130397

ISBN 0-929-70906-3

FAMOUS FOOTSTEPS™

guide booklets
about famous people
in their favorite places

Titles available:

Kit Carson in the West - $4.95
Emily Dickinson in Amherst - $4.95
Lawrence Ferlinghetti in San Francisco - $7.95
Ernest Hemingway in Idaho - $7.95
Ernest Hemingway in Key West - $7.95
John Fitzgerald Kennedy in Massachusetts - $4.95
Jack London in California - $4.95
Marilyn Monroe in Hollywood - $4.95
Georgia O'Keeffe in New Mexico - $7.95
Mark Twain in the U.S.A. - $4.95
Tennessee Williams in Key West and Miami - $4.95

For retail orders contact your:
Local Bookstore
Amazon.com
Baker & Taylor
Barnes & Noble

For comments, suggestions and wholesale
orders contact:
The Computer Lab
P.O. Box 4300, Ketchum, Idaho USA 83340
Phone (208) 726-4717 or fax (208) 726-8413

Table of Contents

Note To Readers

I hope that readers will find this brief guide to Ernest Hemingway in Key West helpful. The worldwide celebration of the Hemingway Centennial in 1999 has verified Hemingway's importance and stimulated interest in both his work and life.

Several of Hemingway's most popular works were produced during the Key West period, from 1928 to 1939. Despite recent gentrification and extensive development, the town has retained the aura of its previous end-of-the-road, outsider, outlaw, renegade attitude. This independently minded community refers to itself as the Conch Republic. Even today a visitor to Key West can experience many of the things which first attracted Hemingway: sea, sun, fishing, boating, swimming, bicycling, eating and drinking. Also entertaining is observing the motley crew of assorted characters from all parts of the world who can be found in the bars, on boats and at the beaches.

Suggested readings by Hemingway evocative of this area include: *To Have and Have Not* (unlike the movie version, the book's locales are Key West and Cuba), *Islands in the Stream* and *The Old Man and the Sea*, which helped him win the Nobel Prize for literature in 1954.

I would like thank all of the people who have been helpful with this project. Those deserving special mention include: Joan and Wright Langley, John Boissonault, Jack Hemingway, Michael Reynolds, Michael Whalton, Bernice Dickson, Mrs. Toby (Betty) Bruce, Benjamin Bruce, Arthur Valladares, Tom Hambright, Linda Larson, Sharon Wells, Jo-Ellen Collins and Tom Oosterhoudt. I especially want to thank my husband, T. Harold Johnson, who also did several of the illustrations for this edition.

Sincerely,
Marsha Bellavance

Chronology

1899 - Born in Oak Park, Illinois, on July 21
1917 - Graduates from high school
        Starts work for *Kansas City Star*
1918 - Goes to Italy for Red Cross and is wounded
1919 - Returns to Oak Park as prohibition begins
1920 - Sells stories to *Toronto Star*
1921 - September 3, marries Hadley Richardson
1922 - In Paris meets Pound and Stein, travels and writes
1923 - Son John born in Toronto in October
1926 - Scribner's publishes *The Sun Also Rises*
1927 - Divorced from Hadley; married to Pauline Pfeiffer
1928 - Arrives in Key West
        Son Patrick born in Kansas City in June
        Suicide of father in Oak Park in December
1929 - Publication of *A Farewell to Arms*
1931 - Son Gregory born in Kansas City in November
1933 - African safari
1937 - Publication of *To Have and Have Not*
        Journalist in Spanish Civil War
1939 - First trip to Sun Valley, Idaho in September
1940 - Publication of *For Whom the Bell Tolls*
        Divorced from Pauline; married to Martha Gellhorn
        Move to *Finca Vigia*, just miles from Havana, Cuba
1944 - Covers WWII for *Colliers*
1946 - Divorced from Martha; married to Mary Welsh
1952 - Publication of *The Old Man and the Sea*
1954 - Second African safari; two plane crashes
        Nobel Prize for literature
1958 - Purchases home in Ketchum, Idaho
1959 - Celebrates 60th birthday with party in Spain
1961 - Gets shock treatments for depression at Mayo Clinic
        Dies in Ketchum, Idaho, on July 2

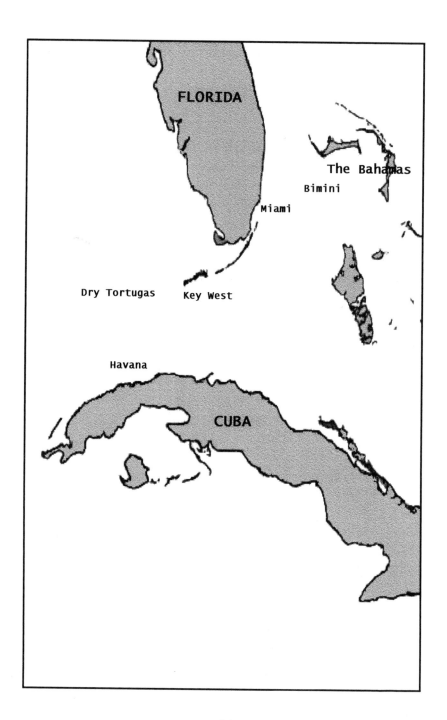

FLORIDA

The Bahamas

Bimini

Miami

Dry Tortugas   Key West

Havana

CUBA

Brief Biography

Ernest Miller Hemingway was born on July 21, 1899, in Oak Park, Illinois, a suburb of Chicago. He was raised in a strict upper-middle class household and had an older sister and eventually four younger siblings, three of them girls. He would always have close and complicated relationships with women. His father was a medical doctor and his mother had trained as an opera singer, so there was always plenty of "proper" cultural exposure. Teddy Roosevelt, Rudyard Kipling, Ring Lardner, and Mark Twain were heroes and role models.

Ernest's travels started at the age of seven weeks when he was taken by various boats and trains to northern Michigan. He was baptized as a Protestant after returning from that trip. It was a trip that he would make many times while spending his childhood summers at the family cottage on Lake Walloon. There he hunted, fished, swam, camped, hiked, canoed and met real Indians. His father, the doctor, taught him natural history, and he acquired a life-long love of nature and the outdoors. Although Ernest never wrote about Oak Park, he later embellished his Michigan knowledge and adventures into successful short stories such as "Indian Camp" and "Up in Michigan."

At school he was a good student and an outstanding writer who worked on both the high school newspaper and literary magazine. He was a keen observer and was able to learn things quickly. Despite his poor eyesight and lifelong susceptibility to illness and injuries, he was also an athlete, a member of both the high school football and swimming teams and an aspiring boxer, too. So, even before his high school graduation he had developed interests in fishing, hunting, swimming, camping, boxing, writing and reading.

His parents wanted him to go to college but, with his uncle's help, he got a job as a cub reporter with the

Kansas City Star. It was there that he was first exposed to criminals, politicians, death, perversions, and the under classes which were conspicuously absent from view in Oak Park. He became adept at portraying deviant, excessive or aberrant behavior to a largely middle-class audience. He was a good reporter and would be involved with some aspect of journalism for the rest of his life.

By 1918 the lure of World War I was irresistible and Hemingway volunteered for the Red Cross. He was wounded while on duty as an ambulance driver in Italy. The newspapers reported that Hemingway had dozens of pieces of shrapnel in his own legs but had heroically carried another man to safety. Seriously injured, he received a sacramental blessing from a Catholic priest, which he later viewed as his baptism. While recovering from his wounds in Milan, he fell in love with his beautiful nurse, Agnes von Kurowsky. In spite of, or because of, his brush with death he enjoyed drinking and got into trouble at the hospital when liquor bottles were discovered in his wardrobe. Before he returned to Oak Park he and Agnes made plans to reunite and marry.

Back home, Ernest was somewhat of a celebrity as a wounded war hero, and he even made a few slightly enhanced speeches about his adventures. But he was shattered when Agnes wrote and informed him that she was engaged to someone else. Later, he used these experiences in love and war as the basis for his novel, *A Farewell to Arms.*

His parents still wanted him to go to college, but he took a temporary job as a tutor in Toronto. Always a voracious reader, he quickly became almost an expert in any subject that interested him. In Canada he was able to get a few articles published by the *Toronto Star.* Hemingway returned to Oak Park, then went to Michigan where he was at loose ends. He was in conflict with his mother, who felt his drinking, swearing, and laziness were a bad example for the four younger children. The day after his twenty-first birthday, his mother kicked him out of the family cottage. The incident can explain some of the hostility he always felt for his mother.

Hemingway then moved to prohibition-era Chicago and stayed with friends while working at a small political magazine. He was interested in several women, including Hadley Richardson of St. Louis, who was eight years his senior and had attended Bryn Mawr College. They exchanged letters and visits and were married in Michigan on September 3, 1921, honeymooning at the family cottage. They saved as much money as possible and with Hadley's small trust fund were planning to go to Italy where Hemingway had heard the living was cheap.

Hemingway, however, had met noted writer Sherwood Anderson, who recommended Paris. When Hemingway got a job with the *Toronto Star's* Paris office, the couple was soon there. With Anderson's introduction to the literary set, Hemingway became a part of the scene which included Sylvia Beach, Ford Maddox Ford, Gertrude Stein, James Joyce, F. Scott Fitzgerald and poet Ezra Pound. By coincidence, Pound was born in Hailey, Idaho, only a few miles from Ketchum where Hemingway would eventually live and die.

While trying to learn to write fiction, Hemingway traveled to Switzerland, Turkey, Italy and Greece, covering events and writing features for the *Toronto Star*. In Paris he enjoyed boxing and attending the bicycle races. Although his earnings were small, by saving on necessities and taking advantage of favorable exchange rates, he and Hadley were able to ski in Switzerland and Austria and tour Spain. In Spain Hemingway was fascinated with the bullfight, which he considered a tragedy, one of the last places where one could observe violent death. As he wrote, "The tragedy is the death of the bull." He would eventually write three books and many articles about bullfighting.

In early 1923, Hemingway and Hadley had been

surprised by her unexpected pregnancy; Hemingway considered himself too young for fatherhood. The couple decided to return to North America and Hemingway got a job with the *Star* in Toronto where they planned to stay for a year. His first son, John "Jack" Hadley Nicanor Hemingway, was born in Toronto in October, 1923. He was named Nicanor after a popular Spanish bullfighter but often referred to by his nickname "Bumby."

Ernest disliked working at the *Star,* so the young family returned to Paris only four months after leaving. It was in Paris that Ezra Pound, Scott Fitzgerald, and Gertrude Stein helped Hemingway to develop as a writer. Pound was also promoting him with some of the small presses and Hemingway was finally starting to get his poems and short fiction published. But back at home his parents were horrified at the language and depraved nature of his subject matter. In fact Hemingway always resented censorship. His publishers frequently required him to edit controversial words and expressions out of his works.

In Our Time and *The Torrents of Spring,* a parody of his former mentor, Sherwood Anderson, established him as a writer. The 1926 publication of *The Sun Also Rises,* about the bullfights and the fiesta of San Fremin in Pamplona, Spain, catapulted him to fame. He had also signed on with Charles Scribner and Sons, who would be his publishers until he died.

As his writing career solidified, his marriage dissolved. Hemingway, a man with four sisters, always enjoyed being surrounded by adoring women. He had fallen in love with Pauline Pfeiffer, an American heiress who worked for *Vogue* in Paris. It seems that as the moral boy from Oak Park, he felt he had to marry the woman he loved, but he was not always sure who he truly loved. Finally, Hemingway and Hadley were divorced and he married Pauline in May, 1927. By April of 1928, Pauline was pregnant, and the Hemingways returned to the United States via Havana and Key West. It was an inexpensive route and would enable Hemingway to visit the Keys, which had been recommended to him by his longtime friend, fellow author John Dos Passos.

They were delayed in Key West. A brand new Ford, a gift from Pauline's rich uncle Gus, was supposed to be waiting for them. Since it was late, they stayed at the Trevor and Morris building, owned by the car dealership (page 29). Ernest immediately got to work on *A Farewell To Arms.* He worked well in the cool mornings and in the afternoons he fished and explored. The Hemingways had no real plans to stay, certainly no more than six weeks. A post war reduction in navy personnel had contributed to the island's population decline from 26,000 to 10,000, and the area was economically depressed. Hemingway liked both the outdoor and outlaw lifestyle of Key West. He had never liked dressing up and in the Keys he could dress casually. He wore a knotted hemp rope belt and sandals with no socks, so he avoided places like the elegant Casa Marina with its strict dress code. He wrote to his editor at Scribner's, Max Perkins, that everybody thought he was a bootlegger or dope peddler since he still had a vicious scar from a Paris accident. He wanted copies of his books sent down to prove that he really was a writer.

Hemingway soon met the local characters who were to become his life-long friends: George Brooks, Charles Thompson, Captain Eddie "Bra" Saunders, and "Sloppy Joe" Russell. Frequently visitors from Paris, childhood friends, and family enlarged the group known as the "Key West Mob." Josie Russell owned both a bar and the charter boat, *Anita.* Charles Thompson, owner of the hardware store, was an insider with the connections necessary to get Ernest and his mob into the Navy Yard (page 35) for swimming and fishing. These friends had boats, and with them Ernest began his life-long involvement with deep-sea fishing. He was also accumulating literary material. From Captain Bra he heard about the ship, *Val Banera,* and later used it in his story "After the Storm".

He was working on *A Farewell to Arms* in the mornings and swimming or fishing in the afternoons. As was his style Hemingway invited old friends and made new ones who took him out in their boats, taught him deep-sea fishing and told him the local stories. He discovered the Dry Tortugas (page 37). Hemingway liked Key West and his special group of "insiders" so before leaving he had decided to return. When he asked the Thompsons to help him find a house to rent, they thought he was joking.

The obligations of impending parenthood interrupted the Key West stay. Pauline wanted to receive better medical care and to see her family in Piggott, Arkansas. Ernest and Pauline went to Kansas City for the birth of Patrick Hemingway on June 28, 1928. Afterwards, they toured around the country and visited family. They were back in Key West by November. Pauline, Patrick, Ernest, and his sister "Sunny" stayed in a small rented house at 1100 South Street. "Sunny" had come down to Key West to type the final manuscript for *A Farewell To Arms.*

Before the novel could be finished, Ernest went to New York to retrieve his young son Bumby, who had traveled by ship from Paris. Their return to Key West was interrupted by a telegram for Ernest; his father had just died in Oak Park, Illinois. Leaving Bumby on the train to go on to Key West by himself, Hemingway took the night train for Chicago. Back at his childhood home, Ernest learned the horrible truth; his father had killed himself! Dr. Hemingway, Ernest's father, had suffered financial reverses and was ill with kidney disease and diabetes. Nonetheless, Ernest blamed his mother and uncle for the suicide, which was a terrible shock to him. Now he felt added responsibility for his mother, brother, and sister, and started to send them money regularly.

Hemingway returned to Key West and immediately

began his revisions of *A Farewell to Arms*. He worked six hours a day, and with Sunny typing, he finished the final draft on January 22, 1929.

In the spring of 1929 his old friends, Scribner's editor Max Perkins and writer John Dos Passos, visited Key West and pronounced the manuscript magnificent. Hemingway took his friends on a boat trip to the Dry Tortugas. Eventually his friendships with other writers such as Dos Passos, Sherwood Anderson, Scott Fitzgerald and Gertrude Stein would disintegrate. This might have been caused by Hemingway's very competitive nature, which even extended to writing.

In April, 1929, the Hemingways went to Paris. They spent the rest of the year living in Paris and traveling in Spain, where they revisited Pamplona and followed the bullfighting circuit. Ernest was working on a bullfighting article for *Fortune Magazine* which he hoped to turn into a book (*Death in the Afternoon.*) Meanwhile, Scribner's had published *A Farewell to Arms* in September, 1929, and it sold 28,000 copies by mid-October.

In January, 1930, the Hemingway's were back in Key West, where Hemingway settled into his routine of writing, fishing, and carousing. The family left for Wyoming in the summer. There Hemingway continued to work on the bullfighting book and made plans for an African safari. On the return trip to Key West in November, Hemingway broke his arm in a car accident. He spent seven weeks in a Montana hospital. The experience formed the basis for his short story, "The Gambler, the Nun and the Radio".

Hemingway continued his recovery in Key West. Most days centered around fishing trips with friends. Despite Pauline's second pregnancy, the Hemingways decided to follow the Spanish bullfighting circuit from May to September, 1931.

Before leaving Key West, they had purchased the dilapidated coral stone mansion at 907 Whitehead Street that was to be their home (page 43) for the following decade. Pauline's Uncle Gus bought the $8000 house as a gift for them. After travels in Europe and the birth of Gregory in November, the enlarged family returned to Key West and moved into their home.

Despite the chaos of a new house and new baby, Hemingway immediately went to work finishing *Death in the Afternoon*. Because of the Depression he had to postpone his plans for an African safari, but he made several fishing expeditions to Cuba with Joe Russell on the *Anita*. From then on, Cuba (page 41) had a special place in Hemingway's affections. In the summer of 1932 he returned to Wyoming. His Key West buddy, Charles Thompson, arrived in the fall, and they went big game hunting, each getting a bear. After family visits, everyone was back in Key West by January of 1933.

With prohibition over, Joe Russell opened his original, legitimate bar, "Sloppy Joe's" (page 31), which kept him too busy for much fishing. Hemingway began work on the Harry Morgan stories, which later formed the basis of the novel *To Have and Have Not,* in which the character of Joe Russell (called "Freddy") is so significant. Hemingway also continued plans for the African trip.

Finally the African safari became a reality. It was bankrolled by a gift of over $25,000 from Pauline's uncle Gus. Ernest, Pauline and Charles Thompson spent the end of 1933 and several months of 1934 in Africa. Ernest was somewhat disappointed, however, since Charles returned to Key West with the prize trophy of the hunt. Nonetheless, Charles is used as the character, "good ole Karl" in the safari book, *The Green Hills of Africa*. Two of Hemingway's most popular stories. "The Short Happy Life of Francis Macomber", and "The Snows of Kilimanjaro", were also based, in part, on the African trip.

In May, 1934, Hemingway's new boat, *Pilar,* (page 47) arrived in Key West. From then on, whenever he wanted, he had the mobility to fish in the Gulf Stream, in Bimini and in Cuban waters. Fishing and writing occupied much of the next year and half. By 1935 he was one of Key West's most prominent citizens and his house was listed as a tourist attraction. In September, 1935, a hurricane hit the Florida Keys. Over 577 bodies were accounted for, and Hemingway wrote an angry article about the disaster for *"New Masses"*, a small magazine. He continued writing in 1936, expanding on the Harry Morgan stories.

Also during this period, Ernest had been carrying on a quasi-clandestine affair with Martha Gellhorn, a beautiful blonde journalist he'd met at the original Sloppy Joe's (now Capt. Tony's, page 31) in December, 1936. As reporters they covered the Spanish Civil War in 1937 and 1938. He supported the Loyalist, anti-Franco forces. Hemingway's only play, *The Fifth Column,* is based on this experience. His fame continued to grow and he was on the cover of *Time Magazine* in October, 1937, when the Book Section did a long piece about him, his life and his new book, *The Green Hills of Africa.*

Hemingway and Martha rendezvoused in Sun Valley, Idaho, in September, 1939; Hemingway had been informally invited to the new resort for publicity purposes. The area impressed him and he returned many times during his life. On his first trip, Hemingway worked on *For Whom the Bell Tolls,* his novel about the Spanish Civil War.

The next fall, in 1940, while Ernest and Martha were back in Idaho, Pauline's divorce from Hemingway was granted. Many of their Key West friends disapproved of Hemingway's leaving his family for a younger woman. On their way back east, on November 21, 1940, Ernest and Martha were wed in Cheyenne, Wyoming. The couple lived close to Key West, in Cuba, and Hemingway continued to see his children and maintain his Key West contacts.

During World War II, Hemingway spent most of his time in Cuba and Key West. He worked semi-officially, through the U.S. Embassy in Cuba, patrolling the seas searching for German submarines on his boat, *Pilar*. One of Hemingway's lifelong habits was to use nicknames, and this group was called the "Crook Factory". These experiences were recounted in his book *Islands in the Stream*, which was made into a movie starring George C. Scott.

Then, as a journalist, he covered D-Day and the final Allied push to victory in Europe. It was during the war that he met Mary Welsh, the woman who was to become his fourth and final wife. He divorced Martha and, in March 1946, married Mary.

Ernest and Mary had settled, more or less, at the *Finca Vigia* in Cuba. Even after their wedding, they traveled to Key West to visit his children or to check on the Whitehead Street property. One of those visits was in May, 1953, en route to Africa for Hemingway's second safari.

For the next ten years, the second African safari, deep-sea fishing, European travels, filming *The Old Man and the Sea,* and writing in Cuba kept Hemingway busy. He won the Pulitzer Prize in 1953 and the Nobel Prize for Literature in 1954.

In 1958, Ernest was overweight and had high blood pressure. Furthermore, he had never fully recuperated from the injuries sustained in two plane crashes in one day while in Africa on the second safari. He was excessively worried about his tax situation and finances. He also thought that the F.B.I. was investigating him, which seemed a paranoid delusion at the time. But, recent research has proven that he really was under F.B.I. surveillance. Several of Hemingway's activities drew attention: involvement in the Spanish Civil War, creation of the "Crook Factory" spy operation, and a high profile in Europe at the end of World War II. In addition to these problems, Hemingway had spent the decade living and writing in Cuba where the political situation was rapidly deteriorating.

In 1959 the Hemingways decided to move to

Ketchum, Idaho, where they purchased a house only a short distance from the Sun Valley Resort.

But Hemingway was not well and his health was worse. Besides having high blood pressure, he was treated for depression at the Mayo Clinic. There were several incidents that seemed to indicate suicidal tendencies. Worst of all, he feared that he had lost his ability to write. The plane crashes, drinking, hard work, hard play and sometimes hard luck had all taken their toll. Then, in Ketchum, on July 2, 1961, Hemingway took his own life with a shotgun in the little entry-hall room where he liked to work. He is buried in the quaint, small cemetery in Ketchum.

To the world he left a legacy of short stories, articles and novels that changed the style of literature. Today the Hemingway legend lives on.

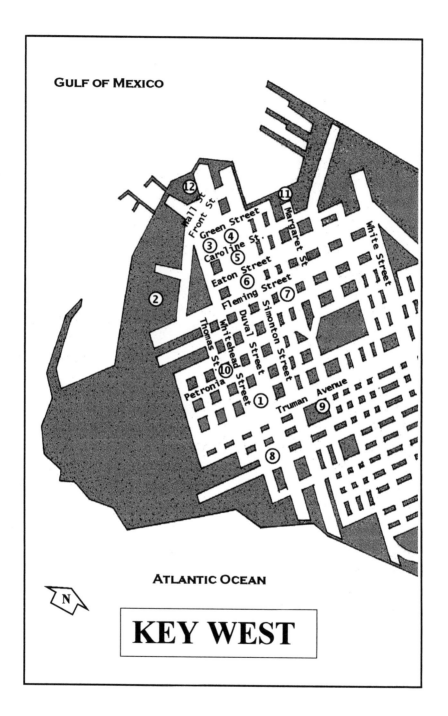

GULF OF MEXICO

ATLANTIC OCEAN

KEY WEST

Map Legend

1 - Hemingway Home and Museum

2 - Navy Yard & Truman Annex

3 - Capt. Tony's

4 - Sloppy Joe's

5 - Casa Antigua

6 - Key West Island Bookstore

7 - Monroe County Public Library

8 - Valladares Newsstand

9 - Saint Mary Star of the Sea Church

10 - Blue Heaven Restaurant

11 - Key West Historic Seaport

12 - Memorial Sculpture Garden

Casa Antigua

The Casa Antigua is almost the same as it was in 1928. The window boxes which have been added overflow with brilliantly colored flowers and provide charm that was absent during the Hemingway's stay. Then it was called The Trev-Mor Hotel/Apartments and was owned by the Ford dealership, the Trevor and Morris Company.

The building, at 314 Simonton Street, still has garages on the first floor. The thick double brick walls kept it cool inside, which was important before air-conditioning.

The young couple stayed in Key West by chance. When the Hemingways arrived they were expecting to have a brand new Ford waiting for them. It was a gift from Pauline's Uncle Gus Pfeiffer. Since the car was delayed, the Ford dealer offered them the company apartment, only a few blocks from the docks. Although it was not at all like the antique-filled apartment that they had just left in Paris, Ernest quickly settled in and began writing.

Hemingway was working on *A Farewell to Arms*. He wrote to his editor that he was doing well with the book and bragged about the tarpon, barracuda and red snappers that he had been catching. Typically, he would work at the Simonton Street rooms in the cool early morning hours. In the afternoon he would explore Key West and environs. The routine of working in the mornings and playing in the afternoons was one that he retained during his entire life. Hemingway quickly made local friends. Soon family and visitors from his "mob" also arrived in Key West. Everyone had a grand time and he decided to return and rent a house.

Today the Casa Antigua building houses the Pelican Poop, a Caribbean Art gallery. From 10-6 daily there are tours of the atrium for only $2. This is also the site of literary readings during the annual Hemingway birthday celebrations held around the week of July 21st. For more information call (305) 296-3887.

Allison Gosney
© '87

Captain Tony's

The oldest active bar in Florida, now called Captain Tony's Saloon, is located at 428 Greene Street, just off Duval. When prohibition ended in 1933, Hemingway's friend Josie Russell opened the first "Sloppy Joe's" bar at this location. Hemingway described this bar in the novel *To Have and Have Not*. In that novel and the Harry Morgan short stories, Hemingway disguised the bar by calling it "Freddy's". In 1937 Russell moved to nearby Duval Street, to a new bar also called "Sloppy Joe's" (page 33).

Captain Tony's is a small, two-story wood frame building which opens onto the sidewalk on Greene Street. During the heat of the day, the doorway seems like a cool black hole in the glaring sun. It has the atmosphere of a place where almost anything could happen. Hemingway usually stopped in at least once a day. One must remember that back then, air-conditioning did not exist. The attraction of a cool, dark bar for an icy drink is obvious. Hemingway's favorite was a mixture of Cuban rum with fresh lime, grapefruit, and maraschino juice, called a "Papa Doble".

It was here, in December of 1936 that Ernest met writer and journalist Martha Gellhorn. She was a political activist, involved in covering the Spanish Civil War, and familiar with Hemingway's writings. She was also blonde, beautiful and young. Gellhorn was traveling with her mother and brother. So refined a group in such a bar soon attracted Hemingway's attention. There is some controversy about whether Martha went to the bar hoping to meet Hemingway. Anyway, she was there and it's where their romance began. It was a meeting that profoundly changed his life since he eventually married her!

Years later, writers Tennessee Williams and Truman Capote also drank in this bar, which can still be enjoyed by visitors today. Call (305) 294-1838 for more information.

Allison Gosney © '87

Sloppy Joe's

On May 5, 1937, Joe Russell moved his popular bar to a new location at 201 Duval Street. For the past sixty years it has remained essentially the same. Now the music is electronically amplified and there's a counter which does a brisk business in Hemingway memorabilia. The bar also sponsors events during the annual July Hemingway birthday celebrations. For information, call (305) 294-5717.

Hemingway seemed fascinated by the characters who drifted into Key West. Those who found their way into Sloppy Joe's were an eclectic assortment of wealthy tourists off their yachts, war veterans, sailors or just thirsty travelers from parts unknown. It's not surprising that Russell and the 300 pound black bartender, Skinner, sometimes needed a sawed-off billiard cue to maintain order. Hemingway sat at the island's longest bar for hours absorbing the atmosphere. As his fame increased, there were times when HE was the atmosphere. This is still true today; paintings, photos and other Hemingway items now decorate the walls. The nightlife of Key West played an important part in Hemingway's life. It is well documented that Hemingway enjoyed drinking in the bars, gambling at boxing or at the cock fights and living his life to the fullest.

Russell was featured in Hemingway's writings too, as the model for both Harry Morgan and Freddy in the novel *To Have and Have Not*. In real life Russell owned Sloppy Joe's, and the boat *Anita*. In the novel Freddy owns a bar and the boat *Queen Conch!* "Josie" Russell died in Havana in 1941, following emergency surgery during a visit with Hemingway, who was shocked at the loss of his drinking and fishing companion of nearly fourteen years.

Hemingway had stored many things at Sloppy Joe's. In 1962 the items were found and turned over to his widow, Mary. They included royalty checks and manuscripts!

Allison Gosney
© '87

Navy Yard

In 1928, when Ernest Hemingway arrived in Key West, the United States Naval facilities were virtually deserted and manned only by a skeleton crew.

The Navy Yard is conveniently located, only a few blocks from Duval Street and close to town. It was especially handy after Hemingway bought his own boat, *Pilar*, and he was allowed to berth her there, an area not open to the general public. He frequently walked the short distance from his home on Whitehead Street.

Soon after getting to Key West, Hemingway met Charles Thompson, owner of the local hardware store, who became a life-long friend as well as the literary character, "Karl" in *The Green Hills of Africa*. He had the connections to get Hemingway access to the Navy Yard. Friends who visited, such as writer Dos Passos or artist Waldo Pierce, swam there with Ernest. In 1934 Hemingway's younger brother Leicester stayed in the yard aboard his boat *Hawkshaw*. He had sailed to Key West prior to going on to Havana, an adventure he later wrote about in his book *My Brother, Ernest Hemingway*. Also in 1934, Arnold Samuelson, an aspiring writer, got a job sleeping aboard *Pilar* at the Navy Yard docks. He wrote about it in his book, *With Hemingway: A Year In Key West And Cuba*.

During World War Two, this area was manned by the Navy. Later President Truman was a frequent visitor, staying at the so-called "Little White House" (open to the public). During the 1960's, hostilities with a close-by Cuba resulted in a flurry of activity. The area has recently undergone tremendous changes. The Truman Annex Company has developed it, and now the shore is lined with condos, hotels and restaurants. Stand at the waters edge and enjoy the same ocean that Hemingway loved. Part of the property is now a park, the Fort Zachary Taylor State Park.

The Dry Tortugas

The Dry Tortugas are a group of seven tiny islands almost 70 miles west of Key West in the Gulf of Mexico. It was a favorite fishing spot for Hemingway and his "mob".

The islands were named *Las Tortugas* (the turtles) by Ponce de Leon in 1513, but because there was no freshwater they were soon known as the Dry Tortugas. The United States government started construction of the all-brick Fort Jefferson on Garden Key in 1846. A Union military prison during the Civil War, it held four men involved in the Lincoln assassination, but was abandoned in 1874. A harbor light was erected in 1876. By the time Hemingway was fishing from the old docks the area was a wildlife refuge and in 1935, before he left Key West, Fort Jefferson was designated a National Monument.

By May of 1928 Hemingway had assembled his "mob", including Waldo Pierce, John Dos Passos, local friend Charles Thompson, and even Pauline's father, for a trip to the Dry Tortugas. Charter boat Captain Bra Saunders told a story which Hemingway later turned into the short story, 'After the Storm." A trip in 1932 included Archibald MacLeish, artist Mike Strater and Pauline's uncle Gus.

For tourists, a visit to the Dry Tortugas is available on a variety of commercial trips by boat or seaplane from Key West. In 1992 the Dry Tortugas National Park was created to protect the historical and natural features of the area. Between March and September over 100,000 sooty terns use nearby Bush Key for nesting. The historic fort is open for touring and there are a few campsites for those who plan in advance. Visitors must bring everything they will need as there are no phones, services or facilities. It's perfect for snorkeling, swimming, fishing, reading, sunbathing, picnicking and photography. Heading back to Key West as the sun is setting is a true Hemingway type experience.

Blue Heaven Restaurant

Friends, family and business associates were constantly traveling around the world to visit Hemingway. In Key West they were known as his "mob". With Pauline and the children at home, Hemingway's mob frequently ate out in one of Key West's many eating establishments. The popular Blue Heaven Restaurant at Petronia and Thomas Streets has housed many business in its more than 100 years of existence: bar, billiard hall, ice cream parlor, dance hall, bordello, and playhouse. In the yard there have been cock fights, gambling and Friday night boxing matches sometimes refereed by Ernest Hemingway, a boxer himself. He first wrote about boxing for his high school paper and he participated in or watched the sport until the end of his life. Hemingway had a ring in his yard and sparred with local fighters. Until their recent deaths, two of these fighters, James "Iron Baby" Roberts and Kermit "Shine" Forbes participated in the Hemingway Days Writers' Workshop and Conference. First hand accounts of their experiences can be found in *Remembering Ernest Hemingway*, by James Plath and Frank Simons.

Today roosters roam freely around tables under lime, coconut and almond trees. A hand painted sign proclaims that the "Rooster Cemetery is the oldest burial ground for cocks on the island. Hemingway buried his here often." The restaurant is open for breakfast, lunch and dinner seven days a week. Bicycles are usually parked outside, in this area of Key West that seems less touched by time.

Mrs. Rhoda Baker's (nicknamed "Rutabaga") Electric Kitchen at 830 Fleming Street was a real favorite, especially for hearty breakfasts, as well as for lunch and dinners costing fifty cents or less. In the same building today, Flaming Maggie's Books, Art & Coffee doesn't serve any food, but does have books and beverages.

Ambos Mundos Hotel

The lovely pink Spanish Colonial style Ambos Mundos Hotel in Havana is a reminder of how different relations between Cuba and the United States once were. Less than ninety miles from Key West by ferry, a trip to Havana was once pretty commonplace for Key Westers. A few months before Hemingway's arrival, in January of 1928, Pan American World Airways began regular passenger service to Havana. When Hemingway returned to the United States from Europe, with his pregnant second wife Pauline, he transited through Cuba. It was a convenient, inexpensive ocean crossing route, with regular connections to Key West.

The Havana/Key West nexus, the contrast of custom, culture and law is part of the dynamic tension in Hemingway's economic political novel, *To Have and Have Not*. He wrote parts of the book in his usual room, on the fifth floor of the Ambos Mundos Hotel. Today the Hemingway room is preserved as a mini-museum, with a glass case displaying his boots and typewriter. He was also a patron of both the lobby bar and roof-top restaurant. Hemingway felt comfortable in the Spanish culture: he spoke the language and had traveled in Spain and written about bullfighting.

It's hard to imagine Hemingway staying in isolated Key West without the conveniences of Cuba, a short boat trip away. And with prohibition in the United States the hard drinking Hemingway especially appreciated the flowing liquor and cosmopolitan atmosphere of Havana.

All through the thirties, while he was living with his wife Pauline in Key West, he, they and their friends were frequent guests at the Ambos Mundos. Later he lived with both his third and fourth wives just a few miles from Havana, at the *Finca Vigia*, now the *Museo Hemingway*.

Hemingway is a heroic figure in Cuba and his legend and history have been appropriately preserved.

ALLISON GOSNEY
© '89

Hemingway Home

Just before Christmas in 1931, Ernest, Pauline and their children moved into the un-renovated old coral stone mansion that was to become their home.

The house is located at 907 Whitehead Street, one block from Duval Street. It was built in 1851 by Asa Tift, a wealthy shipping magnate. The coral was quarried at the site and the hole became the basement. It's a Spanish Colonial style with floor to ceiling windows, opening onto porches which circle the building on both levels. Today, it has the aura of a cool, secluded mansion, surrounded by lush vegetation. When Pauline first saw it, there was no fence, only a few palms and many much needed repairs. Title was transferred to Hemingway on April 29, 1931, for eight thousand dollars, a gift from Pauline's Uncle Gus.

Eventually Pauline refurbished the home. The décor was a blend of her European antiques and fine oil–paintings with animal trophies and artifacts from their world-wide trips. Landscaping and a pool were added and a brick wall built to discourage sightseers who were attracted by Hemingway's increasing fame. The Hemingways spent many happy years in this home. Ernest was able to escape to his workroom (page 45) to write or to the ocean to fish.

When Hemingway left Key West, his family continued to live in the home. It was sold after Hemingway died in 1961. Even now the famous "Hemingway" cats still roam the grounds. One legend has it that a poor spinster neighbor, Miss Marie Chappick, took in numerous cats. Those cats adopted the 907 Whitehead Street home after "Papa" Hemingway started feeding them.

Today the Hemingway Home and Museum is a Registered National Historic Landmark open daily from 9 a.m. to 5 p.m. The admission is eight dollars and includes a tour. For information, see their website or call (305) 294-1136.

Allison Gosney
© '87

The Workroom

Ernest Hemingway found a near-perfect spot for writing when he converted the second floor of a small outbuilding behind his home at 907 Whitehead Street (page 43) into his private workroom. Typically, he rose in the early morning and crossed over to work on a second story cat-walk which connected his study to the house. Today the cat-walk is gone, but the workroom remains. It is similar to the way it was when Hemingway penned his best-selling novels there, and is included on the Hemingway Home tour.

The walls of the spacious room are a showcase for mounted African game trophies. In Key West, and later in Cuba and Ketchum, both animal trophies and books were a dominant feature of his home decoration. Even when he traveled he carried quantities of books. When he settled into his Key West home he had the bookshelves built.

Here Hemingway worked on *Death in the Afternoon, Green Hills of Africa, To Have and Have Not, For Whom the Bell Tolls,* his play *The Fifth Column,* and many short stories such as "Snows of Kilimanjaro". In this room Harry Morgan, Francis Macomber and Robert Jordan were developed by the mind of Ernest Hemingway into characters known the world over.

The pool next to the workroom was built by Pauline for Ernest in 1937. It was fed by salt water and was the first pool in Key West. Since it cost over $20,000 to build, a symbolic "last penny" was imbedded in the concrete. Ernest said it took his last penny to build! But the pool, which Pauline hoped would encourage Ernest to stay home, became an excuse to leave. When working on *For Whom the Bell Tolls,* in 1937, he wrote to a friend that the pool bothered him. The noise came up like a "sounding board", he complained. Now the setting is tranquil, with large Banyan trees and a yard full of exotic flowers, trees, and plants.

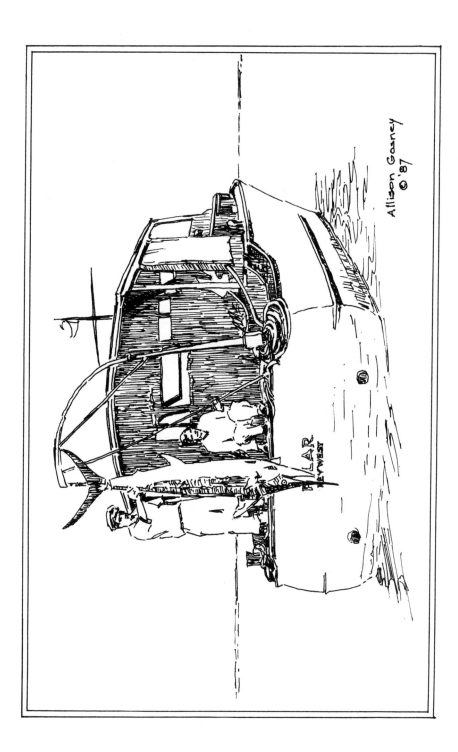

The Pilar

Hemingway began fishing from boats off Key West, in the Dry Tortugas, in 1928. His local friends, Captain Bra Saunders, Sloppy Joe Russell, and Charles Thompson, owned the boats they used. Russell's *Anita* was chartered for marlin fishing excursions in the Gulf Stream. From that time on, Ernest dreamed of owning his own boat.

In 1934, he was in New York, returning to Key West from his African safari. While there, Arnold Gingrich, editor of *Esquire*, gave him a $3300 advance for some short stories. That money became the down payment for his new boat, built at the Wheeler Shipyard in Brooklyn. It was thirty-eight feet, black, diesel-powered, with a galley, sleeping quarters, and two engines: a 75hp Chrysler and 40hp Lycoming for trolling. He named her *Pilar*, once his nickname for Pauline and also the name of the heroine in *For Whom the Bell Tolls*. He docked her at the Navy Yard (page 35), only a short distance from his home.

The *Pilar* provided Ernest with the freedom and mobility he loved. He spent afternoons, days - even weeks - at a time out on the Gulf Stream. But Ernest's interest in fishing had an intellectual side too. He invited two scientists from the Academy of Natural Sciences of Philadelphia to go out and study marlin with him every day for a month and was involved in the scientific classification of the species.

Later, Spain and Martha Gellhorn interrupted his maritime adventures. During World War Two, when he lived in Cuba, the *Pilar* patrolled the Gulf Stream, equipped with electronic gear. Ernest and the crew were looking for German submarines. In *Islands in the Stream* he wrote a fictionalized version of that episode.

The *Pilar* was a boat, a hideout, a research vessel, a spy ship, and finally, a museum piece at the *Finca Vigia*, now the *Museo Hemingway*, outside Havana in Cuba.

Historic Seaport

The Key West Historic Seaport entrance is at the corner of Margaret and Caroline Streets. This charming area with a boardwalk and waterfront restaurants overlooks docks filled with commercial fishing and charter boats.

On the waterfront, The Half Shell Raw Bar with its casual honky-tonky atmosphere and "eat it raw" motto is a local institution. The Turtle Kraals is also a casual eatery named after the pens which were used to hold turtles waiting to be slaughtered. The local cannery produced a green turtle soup. Historic Thompson's Fish House is now an art gallery and operating shipwright, shown in the drawing. From this dock the Yankee Freedom provides daily ferry service to the Dry Tortugas (page 37), three hours and sixty-eight miles away in the Gulf of Mexico.

Because of its deep water harbor and strategic location near the shipping lanes leading to the Panama Canal, in the early 1900's, Key West was Florida's largest city. Standard Oil millionaire Henry Flagler started the Florida East Coast Railroad to connect Miami with Key West, 128 miles away. After seven years and $30 million the first train arrived on the Key West Extension in January of 1912, but failed to live up to its money making expectations. Visitors can relive that time at the Flagler Station Over-Sea Railway Historeum at the entrance to the Seaport. A real railway car, photos and films depict the railroad's history from glamorous beginning to grim end. The railroad was destroyed in the Labor Day hurricane of 1935. During the storm, a train sent to rescue veterans was washed off the tracks. Approximately 600 veterans died. A horrified Hemingway wrote an article for the *New Masses* blaming Washington bureaucrats for the tragedy. By 1938 the Overseas Highway replaced the railroad and connected Key West to the mainland, bringing more tourists and changing the Keys forever.

Saint Mary's

The Saint Mary Star of the Sea Roman Catholic Church is located at Truman Avenue and Windsor Lane. Built of stone with two spires, it may be the very church Hemingway was referring to in chapter 22 of *To Have and Have Not*, when he wrote, "the pressed stone church; its steeples sharp, ugly triangles against the moonlight."

Hemingway had an unusual relationship with the Roman Catholic Church. He had been baptized and later married to his first wife, Hadley Richardson, as a Protestant. But when he wanted to marry the very Catholic Pauline Pfeiffer he convinced Church officials that after his wounding in Italy a Catholic Priest had baptized him. His first marriage was therefore declared invalid as it had not taken place under Catholic auspices and he and Pauline were allowed to marry in a Catholic ceremony in Paris.

Thus Hemingway arrived and lived in Key West as a Catholic. On January 14, 1932, his son Gregory was baptized at Saint Mary's and the family attended Mass there when in town. He supported the Church with donations and, faithful to his vow to help raise the children as Catholics, he would get them to Sunday services when he could.

But the Catholic position about birth control was a problem as was the Catholic/fascist alignment in Spain, which he vehemently opposed. He broke with the Church when he and Pauline were divorced and he married writer Martha Gellhorn in a civil ceremony in 1940. But later he continued his informal support of the Catholics. In Hailey, Idaho he bought a new roof for the Church. In 1961, at his funeral in Ketchum, Idaho, an informal Catholic ceremony was officiated by the Reverend Robert Waldmann.

Tennessee Williams is also known to have attended services here. There are two daily Masses as well as Sunday services. Call (305) 294-1018 for specific times.

ALLISON GOSNEY
© '89

Monroe County Public Library

The attractive pink and white Monroe County May Hill Russell Library building is located at 700 Fleming Street. The library traces its origins to 1858, but this building was built in 1958, so it's unlikely that Hemingway spent time here. However, in an extraordinary coincidence, Agnes von Kurowsky, Hemingway's nurse in Italy during World War One, worked at the library for a few years in the early 1960's. She was supposedly the model for Catherine in *A Farewell to Arms*, written in Key West!

Although Hemingway never went to college, he was a voracious reader and always carried many books on his travels. He also spent time researching facts and figures, which were important to him. Another famous author with Key West connections, playwright Tennessee Williams, liked libraries and reading for the escape from reality which they provided. A 1975 contribution from Williams helped support the Tennessee Williams Center for the Literary Arts, marked by a plaque in the library's auditorium.

The library's Florida History Room has an excellent collection of photos, articles and newspapers relating to Key West. Also available are works by most of the famous writers who spent time in the Keys such as Robert Frost, Elizabeth Bishop, Wallace Stevens, Annie Dillard and John Hersey. This is a pleasant, conveniently located, air-conditioned spot for reading and research. The library is open Monday to Saturday from 10 am to 6 pm, until 8 pm on Mondays and Wednesdays and is closed on holidays. Phone (305) 294-8488 for additional information.

Those on a literary pilgrimage may want to investigate the annual **The Key West Literary Seminar,** held in mid-January, which explores contemporary literary topics. Creative writing workshops are also available. Check their website or call (888) 293-9291 for more information.

Bookstores

Soon after his arrival, Hemingway discovered the **Valladares Newsstand**, now located at 1200 Duval Street. The building that housed the Valladares store on Fleming Street is long gone, but another great bookstore, the Key West Island Bookstore is in the same location, at 513 Fleming Street.

Hemingway and his "mob" regularly stopped at Valladares. In *Papa Hemingway in Key West*, James McLendon writes that Hemingway made a deal, and left signed copies of *Men Without Women* and *The Sun Also Rises* to be sold at the store. Arthur Valladares, a young boy at the time, remembered that Ernest's request for out-of-town papers like the *New York Times* or *Herald Tribune* developed into a profitable line for them. The store, at 1200 Duval Street, continues to carry out-of-town papers, magazines, and paperbacks, emphasizing local writers, including most of the Hemingway titles.

The **Key West Island Bookstore** has a truly outstanding Hemingway collection, including rare signed first editions and books about Hemingway and other local authors. It is a great place to browse and check the calendar, as they are frequent sponsors of lectures and author signings. Call (305) 294-2904 for information.

The **Monroe County Public Library** (page 53) also has an extensive Hemingway collection .

Another shop which carries Hemingway related books, cards, photos and assorted memorabilia is located at the **Hemingway Home** (page 43).

Hemingway books which seem especially appropriate for reading in the Keys include: *To Have and Have Not, The Old Man and the Sea,* and *Islands in the Stream*, all of which are also available on video. See the bibliography (page 59) for titles of more Hemingway related books.

ALLISON GOSNEY
© '89

Memorial Sculpture Garden

Hemingway's literary legacy is celebrated in numerous ways in Key West. Check local calendars for readings and lectures, as well as the play, *PAPA*, set in Key West, which is occasionally performed. Also of Interest:

Key West's Historic **Memorial Sculpture Garden** is located in front of the Waterfront Playhouse in Mallory Square. Opened in 1997, the free outdoor Garden displays bronze busts of the people that "made Key West such a very vibrant and important outpost of American culture and folklore." The sculpture of Ernest Hemingway, donated by the Hemingway Home and Museum, is mounted on a pedestal and has a plaque inscribed with a brief biography .

The **Hemingway Days Festival** was started in 1981 by Hemingway devotee Michael Whalton, who developed a wide range of events surrounding the annual Hemingway birthday celebration on July 21. Reflecting Hemingway's personae from hard drinking macho athlete to cerebral chronicler of his generation, the activities range from the silly to literary. On the literary side are readings, book signings, an open mike night, writing workshops and the Lorian Hemingway Short Story Competition. There is also a Marlin fishing tournament and the world famous Hemingway look-a-like contest. Check the web for updated information or call (305) 294-4440. Key West will probably always have some type of Hemingway birthday events.

In addition, a literary pilgrimage to Key West could be centered around the **Key West Literary Seminar** (page 53) held in January, which attracts top caliber writers.

Island City Strolls with Sharon Wells provides unique and personalized tours, usually by foot or bike, of historic architectural highlights as well as the literary landmarks of Key West. Call (305) 294-8380 for information and to make reservations.

Bibliography

Arnold, Lloyd R., *High on the Wild with Hemingway,* Caxton printers, Ltd., Caldwell, Idaho, 1968.

Baker, Carlos, *Ernest Hemingway: A Life Story,* Charles Scribner's Sons, New York, 1969.

Baker, Carlos, ed., *Ernest Hemingway: Selected Letters 1917-1961,* Charles Scribner's Sons, New York, 1981.

Brian, Denis, *The True Gen,* Grove Press, New York, 1988.

Bruccoli, Matthew, J., ed., *Conversations with Ernest Hemingway,* University Press of Mississippi, Jackson, 1986.

Farrington, S. Kip, Jr., *Fishing with Hemingway and Glassell,* David McKay Company, Inc., New York, 1971.

Hemingway, Ernest, *To Have and Have Not,* Charles Scribner's Sons, New York, 1937.

_____, *Old Man and the Sea, The,* Charles Scribner's Sons, New York, 1952.

_____, *Islands in the Stream,* Charles Scribner's Sons, New York, 1970.

Hemingway, Gregory H., M.D., *Papa,* Houghton Mifflin Co., Boston, 1976.

Hemingway, Jack, *Misadventures of a Fly Fisherman,* Taylor Publishing Co., Dallas, Texas, 1986.

Hemingway, Leicester, *My Brother, Ernest Hemingway,* Winchester House Publisher, Inc., Miami Beach, 1980.

Hemingway, Mary Welsh, *How It Was,* Alfred A. Knopf, New York, 1976.

Hotchner, A.E., *Papa Hemingway,* Random House, New York, 1966.

Kert, Bernice, *The Hemingway Women,* W. W. Norton and Co., New York, 1983.

Klimo, Vernon (Jake), and Oursler, Will, *Heming-*

way and Jake An Extraordinary Friendship, Doubleday & Company, Inc., Garden City, 1972.

Langley, Joan & Wright, Key West: *Images of the Past,* Belland & Swift, Key West, 1982.

Lynn, Kenneth S., *Hemingway,* Simon and Schuster, New York, 1987.

McIver, Stuart B., *Hemingway's Key West,* Pineapple Press, Inc., Sarasota, Florida, 1993

McLendon, James, *PAPA Hemingway in Key West,* The Langley Press, Key West, 1984.

Meyers, Jeffery, *Hemingway: A Biography,* Harper and Row, New York, 1985.

Mellow, James R., *A Life Without Consequences, Hemingway,* Houghton Mifflin Company, Boston, New York, London 1992.

Miller, Madeline Hemingway, *Ernie: Hemingway's Sister "Sunny" Remembers,* Crown Publishers, Inc., New York, 1975.

Oliver, Charles M., *Ernest Hemingway A to Z: The Essential Reference to the Life and Work,* Facts on File, Inc., New York, 1999.

Plath, James and Simons, Frank, *Remembering Ernest Hemingway,* The Ketch and Yawl Press, Key West, Florida, 1999.

Reynolds, Michael, *Hemingway: The 1930's,* W.W. Norton & Company, New York, 1997.

_____, *Hemingway: the Final Years,* W.W. Norton & Company, New York, 1999.